BE SAFE ON THE
PLAYGROUND

BRIDGET HEOS   ILLUSTRATED BY SILVIA BARONCELLI

Amicus Illustrated is published by Amicus
P.O. Box 1329, Mankato, MN 56002
www.amicuspublishing.us

Library of Congress Cataloging-in-Publication Data
Heos, Bridget.
 Be safe on the playground / by Bridget Heos ; illustrated by
Silvia Baroncelli.
     pages cm. – (Be safe!)
 Includes bibliographical references.
"A girl teaches an alien from a planet with no gravity how to
be safe on a playground"—Provided by publisher.
   ISBN 978-1-60753-446-4 (library binding) –
ISBN 978-1-60753-661-1 (ebook)
1. Playgrounds–Safety measures–Juvenile literature. I. Title.
 GV424.H47 2015
 796.06'8–dc23   2013032334

Editor: Rebecca Glaser
Designer: Kathleen Petelinsek

Printed in the United States of America
at Corporate Graphics in
North Mankato, Minn.
10 9 8 7 6 5 4 3 2

ABOUT THE AUTHOR

Bridget Heos is the author of more than 60
children's books, including many advice and how-
to titles. She lives safely in Kansas City with her
husband and four children. You can find out more
about her at www.authorbridgetheos.com.

ABOUT THE ILLUSTRATOR

Silvia Baroncelli has loved to draw since she was
a child. She collaborates regularly with publishers
in drawing and graphic design from her home
in Prato, Italy. Her best collaborators are her four
nephews, daughter Ginevra, and organized
husband Tommaso. Find out more about her on the
web at silviabaroncelli.it

You must be the new kid. Is that a picture of your home planet? Did you really float like that? Our planet has more gravity. You'll have to be careful so you don't fall and get hurt.

Don't worry. I'll show you how to be safe on the playground. That area is for the big kids. We have to stay in our area.

This is our slide. How do you go down the slide?

No, you'll hurt your head that way! You have
to use the equipment properly. Go down sitting.

You can't go *up* the slide. You'll get . . .

. . . knocked down.

Let's try the swings. You'll have to wait your turn. Don't stand there! The person on the swing could accidentally kick you.

That's better.
Now it's your turn.

Sit down! And hold on. Remember to use the equipment properly.

Okay, swinging might not be your thing.

How about a game of four square? This stick is a tripping hazard. Let's move it to prevent an injury.

No, don't move the kids out of the way! They're here to play the game. And roughhousing is not allowed.

Let's go climb the jungle gym.

Uh-oh. The equipment is broken. What should we do?

We'd better tell the teacher.
Don't climb on it! You'll get a . . .

PLAYGROUND SAFETY RULES TO REMEMBER

- Wait your turn.
- Go down slides sitting down. Do not climb up slides.
- Sit down on swings.
- Report broken equipment.
- Move tripping hazards off fields before playing.
- Don't play rough.
- Be careful around younger children.
- Play on the equipment for your age.
- Listen to your parents and teachers.

GLOSSARY WORDS

equipment Objects used for a certain purpose.

gravity The force attracting objects toward a large mass, such as Earth. It's what causes people and objects to fall down.

hazard An unsafe object or circumstance.

injury Damage or harm, when part of the body gets hurt.

prevent To stop something from happening.

roughhousing Wrestling, pushing, or playing in a rough manner.

READ MORE

Donahue, Jill Urban. *Play It Smart: Playground Safety. How to Be Safe!* Minneapolis: Picture Window Books, 2009.

Mara, Wil. *What Should I Do?: On the Playground.* Community Connections. Ann Arbor, Mich.: Cherry Lake, 2011.

Raatma, Lucia. *Staying Safe on the Playground.* First Facts. Staying Safe. Mankato, Minn.: Capstone Press, 2012.

WEBSITES

DANGER RANGERS: PLAYGROUND SAFETY
http://www.dangerrangers.com/kids_safety_topic.php?id=43
Read tips, watch videos, and download activities about playground safety.

PLAYGROUND SAFETY FOR KIDS
http://playgroundsafety.org/kids/tips.htm
Get more playground safety tips.

PLAYGROUND SAFETY ACTIVITIES
http://www.playgroundhound.com/kids-zone/playground-safety-activities
Print these worksheets and do the fun activities to learn about playground safety.

Every effort has been made to ensure that these websites are appropriate for children. However, because of the nature of the Internet, it is impossible to guarantee that these sites will remain active indefinitely or that their contents will not be altered.